What About Boy–Girl Friendships?

What About Boy–Girl Friendships?

By
Lester Showalter

Rod and Staff Publishers, Inc.
P.O. Box 3, Hwy. 172
Crockett, KY 41413
Telephone: 606-522-4348

*Copyright 1982
By Rod and Staff Publishers, Inc.
Crockett, Kentucky
41413*

Printed in U.S.A.

ISBN 0-7399-0209-1

Catalog no. 2145

Table of Contents

Dear Youth	9
Maturity Before Mating	17
Discipline Before Dating	33
Study Before Courtship	53
Do You Wonder Why?	63
Study Questions	67

"Remember now thy Creator in the days of thy youth, while the evil days come not, nor the years draw nigh, when thou shalt say, I have no pleasure in them."

Ecclesiastes 12:1

1.

Dear Youth,

You are in a wonderful time of your life—a time of growing, a time of learning, a time of discovery, a time of new powers, a time of rapidly expanding abilities. You can now run faster and lift more than ever before in your life. You have mastered the art of music and now join in with alto, tenor, or bass. You can now talk, read, and write almost like an adult. Already you have been given responsibility and are excited about the prospect of having the privilege to drive a car. It's wonderfully exhilarating.

What About Boy–Girl Friendships?

You are in the springtime of your life. As a youth you can well afford your sunny and breezy personality. You have almost the full potential of adulthood without the cares and responsibilities that crease the forehead and stoop the shoulders of later years. The heat and work of summer is not yet upon you. Yours is the joy of spring.

James Russel Lowell expressed the delightfulness of spring in the memorable words:

"And what is so rare as a day in June?"

Then, if ever, come perfect days."

Those lines may very well be changed to read:

"And what is so rare as a day in Youth?

Then, if ever, come perfect days."

But, not all the days of spring are bright and sunny. Some days the wind blows cold and it rains. And not all the tears and folly of childhood are out of your life either. The brightness of your youth is often marred by foolishness. You catch yourself saying and doing rather childish things.

Dear Youth

Problems and frustrations arise. Your parents, your teachers, the Holy Spirit, and your own conscience condemn and correct you. An awakened feeling of accountability before God for your behavior brings unrest and personal dissatisfaction. You want God, but you also want your own way.

You are eager to have your many adolescent problems over. You are tempted to hurry things. You think, "If only I could quickly grow up and have the uncertainties of youth in the past. If only I could get a job and earn my own money. If only I could have freedom to sit where I wish during worship services. If only I could buy my own clothes, eat the foods I like, and go where I please. I want to act like an adult today."

But consider well the warning of Scripture:

> Rejoice, O young man, in thy youth; and let thy heart cheer thee in the days of thy youth, and walk in the ways of thine heart, and in the sight of thine eyes: but know thou, that for

What About Boy–Girl Friendships?

all these things God will bring thee into judgment. [Ecclesiastes 11:9]

If you were permitted to make major decisions in your teenage years, you would bring yourself much unhappiness. In many ways you are nearly an adult. But since you have not yet had a wide range of experiences, big decisions would lack wisdom if you had to make them now. Your unwise choices today would someday bring you many heartaches. Those blunders you make now would be multiplied many times and their results would be far more serious if you were to make adult decisions today.

Do not spoil your youth by trying to grow up too fast. There are many special joys in youth for you, if you take time to claim them. Enter wholeheartedly into the responsibilities you presently have. By performing these well, you will develop the wisdom and confidence you need for making adult decisions.

But this will take time. You need all of your teenage years to prepare for adulthood. So leave the decisions of later life until

Dear Youth

that time of your life comes.

In no area is this advice more important than in the matter of choosing a life companion. Yet any young people of school age are tempted to begin solving this adult problem while they are still in school. Either they are encouraged by others to develop a boy–girl love affair, or they have an inner desire themselves for this kind of special relationship.

Many young Christians are sincere and faithful, but are too inexperienced and immature to make such decisions. Faithful Christian living while accepting the counsel of the church and home will bring the needed maturity.

You may have already faced a very baffling personal problem. You have discovered a delightful attraction for the company of those of the opposite sex. You actually enjoy talking and working with boys if you are a girl, or with girls if you are a boy. And to have just one person show special interest in you makes you feel very pleased and important. For

What About Boy–Girl Friendships?

another person to think so much of you that he or she would be willing to live with you for the rest of your life, gives you a thrill.

But the adults with whom you must live say no to any such special interest. Your parents say no. The schoolteachers say no. The leaders of the church and your Sunday school teachers join in saying an emphatic *NO!*

But you wish they would say yes. In some respects, the adults seem hardhearted and cruel on this point. What to you seems so lovely and innocent draws such severe frowns of disapproval.

This letter is to help you see this matter the way the adults see it. Surely protests as strong as those voiced against boy–girl interests must have some reasons behind them. God has very definitely intended that the love that leads to marriage and the married life itself be a delightful experience. But there are some very important reasons why young people should definitely restrain this area of their social life. Let us see what these reasons are.

2.

Maturity Before Mating

The Attraction Between the Sexes Is Part of God's Plan

Many teenagers allow themselves to be drawn into a boy–girl interest without *trying* to be disobedient or rebellious. They are simply following a natural, God-given attraction. But they follow this attraction without properly considering why God gave them this attraction and what God wants them to do with this attraction.

God gave the attraction between men and

What About Boy–Girl Friendships?

women so that homes would be established. God's plan for the home is very wise. Newborn children need the love and security of a happily married couple. Before a husband and wife can give this love and security, they must have a strong love for each other and feel secure in each other's company. The strength of the marriage bond is centered around the special love that exists between a husband and his wife. That love is the product of many years of special attention and sharing. That love is so great that the Scripture compares it to the love Christ has for the church. That love is a special gift of God.

The marriage relationship, like the relation between Christ and the church, is very sacred. God planned the attraction between one man and one woman for the purpose of building strong families and stable homes for the healthy nurturing of children.

Any misuse of this sacred attraction is forbidden by Scripture. Uncleanness in the area of sex is of the worst type of sin.

Maturity Before Mating

When is the natural attraction between those of the opposite sex being misused? It is misused when it is pursued for any purpose other than the purpose of God. That purpose is to establish a home for the rearing of children.

Cultivating a special boy–girl friendship is serious business and should never be played like a game or made into a joke. No dating or other special show of affection should be entered into without the specific purpose of discovering God's will in finding a life companion.

God's Plan Requires Mature Persons

And with this as the proper goal of special boy–girl friendship, no school-age youth is mature enough to enter into that special relationship. No one should make any decision leading to the choosing of a life companion until he or she is old enough to take up the responsibilities of married life. A person who

What About Boy–Girl Friendships?

is not old enough to be a husband or wife is not old enough to know the kind of companion he will need.

When children show special attention to a member of the opposite sex, they are lightly esteeming a sacred ordinance of God.

It is easy to see the folly of school-age love affairs when we consider that some youth try to make a decision before they have been born again. If they are not even mature enough to respond properly in accountability to God, how can they ever clearly understand God's will for a life companion?

If young teenagers claim enough maturity to pursue a specialized boy–girl interest, then they should be ready to successfully take up the responsibilities of nurturing children. But, really now, could they take up the responsibilities of nurturing children and make a success of it? Could they provide for the physical, emotional, and spiritual needs of children? Are they wise enough to discipline little ones?

Maturity Before Mating

Do they know how to face the problems of finances, sickness, and scheduling? Are they ready to be responsible for cooking, repairing, mending, and the many other household duties of parents? Maybe they think they would be able, but the fact is, young teenagers rarely even have jobs that would support a family.

On many questions of right and wrong, teenagers need the guidance of their parents and the church. Youth is a time when a young person is learning to consistently cope with carnal impulses and lusts. Maturity in this area is important for successful fatherhood and motherhood in the Christian home. Young people need much discipline and teaching before they can be mature judges of spiritual things.

One mark of a mature person is a wholesome fear to enter into such a far-reaching decision as marriage. An effort to foster boy–girl interest in adolescence is evidence that this fear is lacking. This is proof of immaturity.

What About Boy–Girl Friendships?

In short, a young teenager is hardly able to handle his own needs and problems, without entering into a vow to care for someone else.

Until a person is mature in these areas of his life, he has no right to enter into the serious task of choosing a husband or wife. Many a young man has too early selected a pretty wife to the ruin of his family. For not only was she pretty, but she was also peevish, indulgent, domineering, or lazy. Many a young woman has fallen for a handsome man to discover with regret that he was also unstable, unspiritual, careless, or cruel.

Immaturity and haste blind the teenager to a host of inconsistencies and faults. By their actions they say, "Get her for me; for she pleaseth me well."

A Mistake Can Be Tragic

If you knew you would probably make a mistake in this matter and would have to live

Maturity Before Mating

fifty long years of regret, would you consider it foolish to wait? Youth are very prone to make mistakes in judging the true value of a thing. And since you are a youth, it is absolutely too risky for you to take steps to make that choice now.

The worldly society approves and even promotes early dating. But the world reaps a high rate of broken homes. Too often the teenage married couple discovers too late that they are not really happy with their choice. So they involve themselves in a worse wrong and get a divorce. Homes are broken, children without two proper parents are left insecure, and two lives stand condemned by putting asunder what God has joined.

But in the church, we do not allow divorce. Christians believe their marriage vow before God makes them responsible to each other for life. So a disappointed couple buckles down to endure thirty, forty, or more years of unpleasantness, trying to make the best of it.

What About Boy–Girl Friendships?

But in such cases, the best that can be done is often far from ideal. Differences of opinion and countless frictions arise that are hard to resolve because the father and mother are not really unified and do not really love each other strongly enough.

The children may develop insecurity and emotional problems. They may turn bitter at the hypocrisy they see when Mother puts on a good front to support Father's wishes, and Father does things just to make Mother satisfied. The children will probably lack proper love and good discipline. If such children prove a blessing to their parents and the church, it will be in spite of the home and not because of it. And the results go on and on.

Take Ahab, for example. Did he choose Jezebel for her genuine, good qualities? No indeed! By courting her, he formed a political tie with her heathen father.

But after marriage, she blossomed into a Baal-worshiping, prophet-hating tyrant. By

Maturity Before Mating

this foolish choice, Ahab doomed the whole nation of Israel to idolatry and its dreaded result—captivity.

But the tragedy did not stop with Israel. Jezebel's daughter, Athaliah, married a king of Judah and dragged that nation to ruin also. The effects of Ahab's foolish courtship persist to this very day.

A Mistake Can Limit Usefulness

Let us suppose the teenage friendship does actually result in a loving, peaceful home life. Even then, how many services for God are limited by poor judgment in choosing a companion? The wife may sincerely want to share with others and be rich in almsdeeds, but the husband does not share her giving spirit. A husband may be qualified to be a spiritual leader in the church, but is greatly hindered by his gossiping wife.

Such circumstances suggest the statement "I have married a wife [such as she is], and

What About Boy–Girl Friendships?

therefore I cannot come [to be a minister, missionary, Christian writer, schoolteacher, etc.]."

Some marriage partners seem to live together happily, but they must surely wish they had chosen more wisely. God often salvages some good from the mistake, but its scar is very deep and lasts a long time.

In the light of this, why should you not want to wait another six or eight years to begin seeking your life companion out of fear that you will make a mistake if you rush into a decision now?

Teenage Decisions Do Effect Later Decisions

But some teenager might say, "I am not deciding about a life companion now. I am only learning to know this person better and am enjoying a rich friendship in the process."

But what you do not know is that such a cultivated friendship does tend to bind a person. Understanding and comradeship develop, which are very difficult to break

Maturity Before Mating

later. For one thing, you have feelings that draw you deeper and deeper into the friendship. Even if you later realize your mistake, you may have forged such strong emotional ties that you cannot bring yourself to break the relationship.

Even if *you* later decide to stop the special friendship, you must face the feelings of the other party. Imagine the embarrassment, the difficulty and heartache in terminating such a friendship. You have allowed a growing attachment to develop with all its feelings and dreams. Now you cannot expect the other to break it off without some struggle. He may so beg and appeal to your sympathy that you are sorely tempted to give in against better knowledge. In this way an adolescent attachment can be so strong that it may tug a couple into a foolish marriage.

But you may say, "Many have gone this road and are happily married." First of all, that in no way minimizes the terrible risk.

What About Boy–Girl Friendships?

And second, you probably do not know all the unhappiness that has resulted.

Would you expect disappointed partners to broadcast such information? Telling the public would only make matters worse in such a home. So instead, they suffer silently and appear satisfied to those who observe the family.

God Has a Plan for Your Life

Also, we believe that God has a plan for each of our lives. One requirement in realizing that plan is patience. Those who run ahead of God will surely be going their way without Him. And to go forward without God is to flirt with disaster. Often young people are tempted to run ahead of God's plan while in school.

By the time some young people are out of school, they have never even met the companion God has for them. School-age children often have a very limited contact with young

Maturity Before Mating

people outside their own community.

This does not mean that it is most ideal to get a partner outside one's own community. In fact, good homes are best built when the husband and wife have similar backgrounds, and God usually plans marriages that way. But it is wisdom to give God a chance to open and close the right doors.

God Requires Purity

Let us suppose, for the sake of discussion, that a school-age interest does lead to a marriage that brings happiness and apparent blessing from God. What assurance does the couple have that even then the choice was what God had in mind?

When the times of trial come, as they surely will, the mind will be haunted with the very real possibility that this was not, after all, God's perfect will. A person can stand adversity a great deal better if there is confidence that he is in the perfect will of God.

What About Boy–Girl Friendships?

God is not wholly pleased with a union that started during the early teenage years. For, as many points in this letter reveal, starting a special boy–girl friendship while in school is not wise and is therefore foolish. And God would never lead a person to engage in foolishness. So we must conclude that God did not lead in the beginning of such an early boy–girl interest.

How then can such a couple be sure that God ever did lead? Blinded by their own immature love, they may have thought God was leading, when, in fact, they were only following their own natural impulses. Not everything that seems right *is* right.

So far we have dealt with only one objection to early adolescent love affairs. An adolescent is simply too young and immature to have the wisdom and experience with God's leading to make such a momentous choice.

3.

Discipline Before Dating

The Flesh Must Be Controlled

The second reason for objecting to school-age boy–girl interests is that such relationships fan the flames of emotion and passion at an age when young people should be learning to control them. Strong forces are not controlled by letting them run freely.

The attraction between the sexes is among the strongest physical drives that God has given man. In its rightful place, it contributes to the strength of the home. But like all other appetites

What About Boy–Girl Friendships?

God has given us, if misused, it brings misery and guilt before God. These appetites can be rightly used only when they are controlled.

But control of our bodily appetites does not come naturally. We are not born with self-control. Everyone is born with the tendency to eat too much food and the wrong kind of food. Only the disciplined person can eat and drink to the glory of God.

God provided for many years of parental care to help you develop the proper control of your appetite for food. Sweets are limited; a balanced diet is enforced. You are taught to eat some foods you would rather not taste. And, in general, your times of eating are scheduled. You are not allowed to just follow your whims and fancies.

Your parents know that if you do not gain control over your appetite, you will be unhealthy and will likely shorten your life. Christian parents know that a person sins when he is not moderate in his eating. Therefore, to spare you the heartaches of

Discipline Before Dating

sinful eating, they have disciplined your eating.

And so it is with the attraction between the sexes. This attraction does not appear in children until the early teens. Until then, children associate freely with both sexes or prefer their own sex. But in early adolescence, youth develop a special desire to be appreciated by a person of the opposite sex. This natural appetite or desire must be disciplined.

God Requires Purity

It would be the height of folly to permit this desire for marriage companionship to go undisciplined. The moral laws of God demand control of this passion. For God insists that it is wrong to use the sex attraction in an impure way.

The seventh commandment, "Thou shalt not commit adultery," is a summary of many Old Testament laws related to social purity. Men and women are not to have marriage

What About Boy–Girl Friendships?

relations with any but their own married partner. The New Testament reinforces this principle in many passages.

> Now the works of the flesh are manifest, which are these; Adultery, fornication, uncleanness, lasciviousness. [Galatians 5:19]

The four sins mentioned here all refer to the misuse of the sex attraction.

> Flee fornication. Every sin that a man doeth is without the body; but he that committeth fornication sinneth against his own body. [1 Corinthians 6:18]

Christ clearly exposed the root of adultery. He said,

> Ye have heard that it was said by them of old time, Thou shalt not commit adultery: but I say unto you, That whosoever looketh on a woman to lust after her hath committed adultery with her already in his heart. [Matthew 5:27, 28]

Discipline Before Dating

This is a very searching statement. First, it plainly tells us that matters of sex must not be taken lightly. There must be no trifling with this sacred relationship. Jokes and evil stories about sex stir up the mind to think sinful thoughts. And Christ makes it very clear that even the lustful look is sin.

Second, this statement is very sobering to the person who sincerely wants to do what is right. The flesh has a strong desire to do the very thing that is prohibited. Therefore, a sober-minded teenager will appreciate every help he can get to overcome this temptation. He will cooperate with every effort of his parents, the church, and the school to help him gain control of this area of his life.

It is clear from the Bible that God intends for the emotions and passions of sex attractions to be severely restricted. In giving us the above-mentioned Scriptures, God knew what He was doing. He did not lay down these laws to make it hard for us. He knew

What About Boy–Girl Friendships?

that before this attraction could be a blessing to mankind, it would need to be confined to the marriage relationship.

Broken homes, unwed mothers and fathers, and unwanted children give testimony to the curse of undisciplined young people. Furthermore, several terrible diseases are spread by the sin of undisciplined relationships between men and women.

All use of sex outside of marriage is wrong and leads to some of the worst consequences known to man. And even in marriage, if the partners are not disciplined in this area, it can lead to the terrible hardships of unfaithfulness. God's Word and our observation appeal strongly for self-control.

Impurity Spoils Character and Later Control

The way to gain control of a wild horse is to keep it in very close check until the horse is tamed and has the wild spirit under control.

Discipline Before Dating

Only after rigid control can the reins be slackened some.

In the same way, the sex passions must be kept in strict control when they first appear. The imaginations must not be allowed to roam freely. What the eye beholds must be carefully guarded. Furthermore, no special attraction for a particular person of the opposite sex must be allowed to assert itself. No suggestive talk may inflame the mind. Teenagers hurt themselves terribly when they listen to filthy talk and deal in vulgar words or words with a double meaning. These things break down self-control in an area that can very easily get out of control.

Paul names uncleanness and fornication as being sins that should not be named among Christians. But he does not stop there. He goes on to say, "Neither filthiness, nor foolish talking, nor jesting" (Ephesians 5:4). Jesting refers to telling an evil joke. Students who make a joke of sex and use dirty language to entertain each other are engaging in a serious

What About Boy–Girl Friendships?

wrong. They are polluting one another's minds and making it very difficult to ever have victory over impure thoughts. Is it any wonder that the home, church, and school discipline such behavior and teach strongly against it?

A young teenager simply cannot engage in impurity and gain proper control in time for a wholesome courtship in later teens. If a person wants to have pure thoughts when he is an adult, he must deliberately control his fleshly appetite when he is young. And school-age boy–girl interests work against control in this area. Rather than helping the young person to bring his thoughts into control, they tend to draw the attention to the very direction to be avoided.

Such love affairs very quickly turn to a sensual, physical attraction if, indeed, they are not born out of a physical attraction in the first place. Often it is quite clear that the selection was made on the basis of physical beauty rather than on the basis of Christian character. How can God bless such carnal attractions?

Discipline Before Dating

Young children do not choose on the basis of Proverbs 31. "Favour is deceitful, and beauty is vain: but a woman that feareth the LORD, she shall be praised." If they did, there would be no young girls to flirt with, because any young girl who fears God as she should will not allow herself to be drawn into such a harmful relationship at so early an age. Through faithful teaching in the church and home, she would realize the folly of it as well as her own need for growth and discipline, before entering into such important decision making.

*Courtship Should Begin With
Much Reserve*

If an adolescent friendship develops into courtship, it is likely begun without a very important ingredient. That ingredient is reserve. Properly cultivated self-control brings a wholesome shame and reserve that forbids physical intimacies during courtship. The physical part of the marriage relationship is

What About Boy–Girl Friendships?

held too sacred to be trifled with during courtship.

Courtship is begun with much reserve and with a certain amount of bashfulness and coolness in the relationship. Very little, if any, confiding is done the first several visits. Verbal expressions of appreciation and affection are very guarded and discreet. Conversations are friendly but not too intimate. Neither is sure that this relationship will continue. All is left open to the leading of the Lord, the counsel of parents, and the observations and spiritual judgments the couple make themselves.

Only in this way can the two really look at each other objectively. Once a decision of intended marriage has been communicated to the other party, either spoken or by warmness of actions, they tend to be a lot less critical of the other persons' faults and weaknesses.

Some character faults that should be seriously considered may not show up until after

Discipline Before Dating

several months or longer of the courtship. If the couple already near the beginning has an unspoken understanding that the relationship will most likely continue, they tend to push such observations into the background and concentrate on the much-looked-for evidences of special attention and affection. This is very blinding.

The time to examine a piece of merchandise critically is before you decide to buy it. For once the decision is made, you will be more likely to look for things about the article that will confirm the wisdom of your decision.

So the wise couple deliberately keeps their courtship very tentative. They do this even if they feel strongly attracted to each other. It is a time of testing. It is a time great cautiousness. They approach each visit with the questions, "Will this person be the right companion for me for the rest of my life? Do I want this young woman to be the mother of my children, or this young man to be the

What About Boy–Girl Friendships?

father of my children?" They keep marriage definitely in view. The seriousness of the marriage vow takes away the light-mindedness and makes them very careful.

The true purpose of courtship is very sobering. During that time two persons are seeking the Lord's will for their life companion. This is quite a responsibility. It is no task for immature young people. Much prayer, much counsel, much careful observation, much personal examination, much consideration of the other's strengths and weaknesses, much confronting one another with questions, and much sharing of ideals must precede a wise decision.

For the first while the visits are arranged one at a time, giving an easy way out if either wants to stop the relationship. No large projects are begun at first that would suggest that the relationship was to go on without question. Great care is taken not to appear too settled in the choice. The Lord blesses such earnestness and carefulness.

Discipline Before Dating

Courtship Is Spoiled by Premature Relationships

But, oh, how different it is with the couple who began their friendship in school. The pair has it all made out ahead of time. They have already shared much with each other in a personal way. They both eagerly await the age when they can have their first date. They even communicate with each other about that fact. The one waits until the other is old enough. At the earliest possible date, they rush to be together. Both they and the community expect that it will only be a matter of time until they will be married.

But they are blind to each other. They accept each other as they are and have never put each other to a test. The surprise is gone. The opportunity to discover a new personality is to a large extent missing. There is no need for one's best efforts and great carefulness of expression. It has all been more or less decided beforehand.

What About Boy–Girl Friendships?

One really delightful aspect of courtship is lost to such a couple. There is nothing quite so rewarding in human relationships as to work faithfully to win the confidence of another and to at last win that confidence completely and without reservation. In a proper courtship, the young man is not quite sure of his lady friend's answer until he actually asks her if she will marry him. He fears the question may be asked too soon. So he decides to wait to be able to answer some questions in his own mind. He wants to be very sure of his own decision as well as of a sure answer on her part. But at last he has courage enough to ask.

The couple who began their friendship in their adolescent years never have the extra joy of learning that at long last the friendship is for real. For them, so much is taken for granted. Their eventual marriage is not born out of struggle. And what one does not need to work for is usually lightly esteemed.

Discipline Before Dating

Courtship Should Be a Time of Testing

A young woman should make herself a challenge to win. If she does not, she need not be surprised to learn after the wedding day that the groom did not really want her very badly. Any young man who really wants a young woman to be his wife will gladly work for her confidence. Such a trial will bring the best out of him. Habits will be broken for her sake. Interests will be developed for her sake. Hardships will be borne for her. A man who responds this way will make a good husband.

But a man will likely not get this pruning if it is all made out while in school. And what is more, his wife will sorely miss the refinement in him once they are married.

The real test of his character and how he will treat you after marriage is how he relates to his family now. Does he respect the authority of his father and mother consistently? Does he show respect, kindness, courtesy, and consideration toward all his brothers and

What About Boy–Girl Friendships?

sisters and toward his parents? The same test is valid for the young woman. How does she relate to her family?

A bride should never expect that she will be able to reform her husband after they are married. After marriage the wife must submit herself to her husband. If the young man is not the kind of person she would want to submit herself to before marriage, she will surely find submission a trying duty after marriage. Before marriage is her time to try and test and hold out on him. Only then can she rightly challenge and test him. After marriage, challenging is out of order; then she is to submit.

But you may object, "If she makes herself a challenge to win, she may never get married." But the choice is not just between being married or not being married. It is a three-way choice related to being married to a selfish, inconsiderate person; being married to a faithful Christian; or not being married. Granted, to be married to a faithful

Discipline Before Dating

Christian with the Lord's blessing is indeed a delightful prospect. But if the choice is between a bad marriage or no marriage, then it is better not to be married. Any right-thinking person would make that same choice. Solomon knew which would be better. "It is better to dwell in the wilderness, than with a contentious and an angry woman" (Proverbs 21:19).

And the only way you can truly test the character of a suitor is to make yourself a challenge to win. By this method you can practically eliminate the worst of the three choices.

God's Will Is Better Than Our Wishes

Furthermore, if God wants you to be married, He will see to it that you are indeed married in His own good time. We can have that confidence in Him, and He does not need our early teenage help in the matter.

If God does not want you to be married,

What About Boy–Girl Friendships?

then would you want to be married against His will? Only a carnal, flippant girl or boy would want to be married in spite of God's will. That would be folly.

It is not always God's will that a person be married. Sometimes in His providence, He has plans for greater fulfillment in life outside of marriage than the person could ever realize in marriage. Marriage does tie a person down to home responsibilities. It is not proper for a mother to work away from home. It is not proper for a father to be away from home for long periods of time.

God seems to have special blessings in store for those who serve Him outside of marriage. Paul is, of course, an outstanding example. Today many sister schoolteachers are serving the church in a very honorable way that they could not serve if they were married. Others are very meaningfully serving the aged, the sick, and the handicapped.

Discipline Before Dating

Pure Courtship Demands Discipline

Discipline and restraint are very important for a God-honoring courtship. Restraint and reserve are necessary to be able to keep the courtship pure. Too many otherwise happy marriages are spoiled by sin during courtship. When the dating couple feel too carefree around one another, loose conduct, bodily contact, and physical intimacies result. The restraint cultivated during the early teens will be a good safeguard against indecency during courtship. This restraint is broken down by petty love affairs at school. If the couple have been paying attention to each other for a long time before courtship, there is already a familiarity that breaks down self-control. In general, immature boy–girl interest stimulates carnality and leads to loose morals.

Many reasons point to the fact that the years before courtship should be used for discipline instead of indulging in boy–girl interests.

"*Study to shew thyself approved unto God, a workman that needeth not to be ashamed, rightly dividing the word of truth.*"
2 Timothy 2:15

4.

Study Before Courtship

Boy–Girl Interests Stunt Growth

There is yet a third reason for avoiding adolescent love affairs. Though some may disagree, such interests *do* have a harmful effect on educational and spiritual growth. For those involved, the main attention and interest is not on learning. Special energy and planning go into promoting the relationship. Time is robbed from study to write letters and daydream. The mind is preoccupied with affairs other than school lessons or Bible study.

What About Boy–Girl Friendships?

And the crippling effect surely goes beyond academic lessons to the social and spiritual areas as well. This interest will likely distract the mind during worship and prayer. Often the involved couple will even use public worship services to exchange glances and talk with other young people.

This unwholesome interest also tends to monopolize the conversation when girls are together. "Out of the abundance of the heart the mouth speaketh" (Matthew 12:34). If boys are uppermost in a girl's mind, that is what she will tend to talk about. While the mind could be sharing with others about spiritual things, it is conversing in a morbid way about who likes whom, who broke up, who's getting married, and on and on. The same thing can be true of boys.

At the same time this is going on, the young persons' attitudes toward parents, ministers, and teachers are deteriorating. His general conduct becomes more undisciplined. Punishment results. The teachers

Study Before Courtship

and preachers are accused because they "pick on me." The teenager's character and personality turn sour. The verbal responses become more snappy and ill-tempered. The rebellion that results from disobeying the teaching of the home, school, and church on the matter of boy–girl interest spreads to a general independent and stubborn spirit.

It can no longer be said of the teenager that he is growing in wisdom and stature and in favor with God and man. Although the stature does not stop, the other three things are stunted.

At a time when the teenager should be cultivating a devotion to God and growing in confidence and trust in God, he or she is cultivating a devotion to a person. This works against spiritual growth and hinders prayer. A person cannot expect normal spiritual growth when he is living under God's displeasure.

What About Boy–Girl Friendships?

A Prospective Parent Has Much to Learn When Young

There is so much that needs to be learned that a young person cannot afford to squander his school years with a competing interest. When a person squanders his school experience, he fails to develop into a truly attractive person. The really attractive young person of dating age is that person who has broadened his interests and has knowledge and abilities in many areas. The really useful Christian is that person who has wholeheartedly applied himself to learning while in school. But love affairs tend to be limiting. They narrow one's interests.

Youth should be a time of concentrated Bible study. Although Bible study should continue all through life, youth is especially suited for this. The mind is fresh and clear, the burdens of adult life do not hinder concentration, the memory is good, and there is more time for uninterrupted study. A boy–girl interest greatly hinders one's interest in Bible study.

Study Before Courtship

Also, because a young person is relatively free from obligations, he is free to enter wholeheartedly into service opportunities for extended periods of time. Disaster work, relief work, singing for the sick and old, distributing Gospel literature, and many interesting and unexpected opportunities crop up. The unique opportunities of youth give fulfillment to the Christian life and provide areas of learning and growth.

Service activities greatly broaden the youth's vision for the needs of the world and the church. After the responsibilities of a home and family come, a person is not as free to enjoy such opportunities. Let it be noted that an early marriage cuts such time of preparation short.

Courtship Should Not Begin Too Soon

How old should a person be before he gets married? Many mature Christians believe that a bride and groom should be at least

What About Boy–Girl Friendships?

twenty-one. Twenty-four or twenty-five would allow for even better maturity and more of the needed preparation.

If a couple then should be well into their twenties before they marry, it follows that they should not begin courtship until they near the age of twenty or older. Courtship that extends much longer than two years is generally not wise. Surely school age is much too soon to begin.

A person must have time to evaluate the one he wishes to court. He should, without fail, discuss his interests freely with his parents and seek and take seriously their counsel before he reaches any conclusions. More mature Christians, such as ministers and parents, are able to give safe guidance for sound evaluations.

He should not only scrutinize his prospective friend, but her family as well. True, he is planning to marry only one person. But he will need to relate to the whole family rather closely. Family pressure and practice are very

Study Before Courtship

persistent. Many a young person has been swept off his spiritual moorings by the influence of the family into which he married. Consequently, each young person needs time to gather the advice of his parents and other older people before he begins a courtship.

This kind of evaluation requires much spiritual perception—something that a school student is very much lacking. It also requires observation over a period of many years. How many times do you think the counsel of parents is sought in developing early adolescent love affairs? Little, if any. This serious lack of what should be considered necessary, greatly underscores the foolishness of such interests.

Boy–Girl Interests Create an Unhealthy Classroom

In many ways, boy–girl interests in school develop an unwholesome situation in the classroom. The teacher must be careful with

What About Boy–Girl Friendships?

the seating lest a certain arrangement will provoke teasing from others or actually start a "love affair." A boy must be careful not to talk to a girl in a casual way lest it arouse rumors. Note passing, writing notes in class, whispering in tight circles in out-of-the-way places, and a whole spectrum of uneasiness and carnality can follow.

Jealously among students can also result. Students may sometimes develop spite for mate snitching. In short, not one good thing comes of it.

It is important that young people do develop a wholesome attitude toward those of the opposite sex. They should become acquainted with their interests and special contribution to society. They should learn proper courtesy and the ability to carry on a conversation with ease in their presence.

This social growth is best made in a community that recognizes the wholesomeness of boys and girls associating together in well-supervised situations. This growth is

Study Before Courtship

severely hindered by a community that pushes young people to enter into the role of courtship before they have mastered the basic graces of community living.

If a community is united against school-age courtship and will not tolerate such interests to be demonstrated until a proper dating age, then boys and girls can converse and work together in a wide variety of groups to the social improvement of all. This would be ideal.

Thou wilt keep him perfect peace, whose mind is stayed on thee.

Isaiah 26:3

5.

Do You Wonder Why?

In light of all that has been said on this subject, do you still wonder why your parents, the school, and the church take the stand they do on boy–girl interests? After all, why would any young person allow himself to get involved in such a foolish thing and spoil his own growth and future happiness and that of the other party? Why would any parent promote or tolerate this in even a little way? And why would any teenager be so foolish as to tease others about this interest and in other ways encourage interest along this line?

What About Boy–Girl Friendships?

Shall we not conclude that such a person either desires to bring a fellow youth harm or else he is ignorant of the consequences? I really do not think that in a general way young people want to harm each other. Therefore, we must conclude that there is a basic ignorance on this subject in some church settings. Hopefully, the situation can be corrected. To that end this letter was written.

But even with this letter, we know that there will still be a struggle. Satan, our flesh, and worldly society are united in working against our best interest along this line. We will need the grace of God to have victory. But before God will give us that grace, we will need to want to have a pure teenage life.

So we appeal to you as our beloved young people. If your life is free of the problems discussed in this letter, you have real reason to pray and thank God for giving you grace to stay free of this error.

But if Satan and your flesh are even at this present time trying to defeat you, then

Do You Wonder Why?

you need to pray for victory over this problem. Pray for courage to break off any such relationships. Pray for strength to declare to your friends what your conviction is on the subject when the matter comes up. Commit your life to the providence of God and trust in Him to fulfill His will for your life. "Casting all your care upon him; for he careth for you" (1 Peter 5:7). Pray for interest in your studies and your work so that you might grow and so that your mind can be disciplined. Such an interest will also help you keep your mind from temptation.

Then, secondly, abstain from all appearance of evil. This may require that you develop new friends. This may mean that you will have to overcome a bad habit of speech or conduct.

The going may be hard, but the goal will be worth the effort. It is much better to have a life of rejoicing than a life of regret.

Study Questions

Dear Youth

1. In what ways are you in the springtime of your life?
2. What tends to make a teenager dissatisfied with his present standing in society?
3. Why is it not wise for teenagers to have the freedom of decision making that they often want?
4. What will help teenagers gain the experience they need to make wise decisions?
5. What decision with far-reaching consequences are young teenagers inclined to make?
6. What makes them inclined to make this decision?

Maturity Before Mating

7. What is the purpose of this attraction?
8. How does God look on the wrong use of this attraction?
9. Give three areas of maturity needed before choosing a life companion, and tell in what

Study Questions

   way a teenager is yet immature.
10. What happens to many homes begun before the partners were mature enough?
11. What tragedy results even if two poorly matched persons remain married?
12. How could a poor choice of life companion limit a person's usefulness?
13. In what way do boy–girl interests in school tend to bind a person?
14. Why is it very unwise to be bound by such friendships begun at this age?
15. What should be the main consideration in choosing a life companion?
16. What knowledge will help a married couple bear the stress of family problems?

Discipline Before Dating

17. What must be done to any normal desire of our flesh?
18. What is God's attitude toward impurity?
19. Why should we not listen to or repeat impure jokes and stories?

Study Questions

20. What natural reaping results from undisciplined relations between men and women?
21. What usually motivates a school-age choice for companionship?
22. Why is reserve a quality of prime importance in the choice of a life companion?
23. Why should dating couples not act overly interested at the beginning of courtship?
24. In what way is a person hindered in evaluating another if the choice is considered as good as final?
25. What is the real test of a young person's character?
26. What is worse than not being married?
27. For what reason might a person decide not to marry?

Study Before Courtship

28. Why do boy–girl interests in school hinder academic work?
29. Why do boy–girl interests in school hinder spiritual growth?

Study Questions

30. What relation is there between boy–girl interests in school and poor attitudes and misconduct?
31. What three things should a young person put his energies into to prepare himself for adult life?
32. Describe what ought to be true of the social relationships in an ideal school classroom.

Since 1960, Rod and Staff Publishers, Inc., has continued to produce sound Christian literature—the kind of reading material that strengthens Scriptural convictions, aids witnessing, and is vital to happy home relationships.

Call or write for a free catalog:

Rod and Staff Publishers, Inc.
P.O. Box 3, Hwy. 172
Crockett, Kentucky 41413
Telephone: 606-522-4348

The Priceless Privilege and Other Stories

Lucy Conley. Rosemary's search for truth brings her face to face with such questions as What is right? Who is right? How can anyone know? Tempted to leave the unhappy church her family attends, and influenced by an active young man who seeks her friendship, Rosemary longs to associate with true people of God. Will she ever find such a church? 23 stories for youths and adults. *242 pages.*

Dear Princess

Mary M. Landis. Do you have problems with personality, your temper, those anguished feelings of self-pity? Do you have problems making friends? Is your Christian life an up-and-down, boring experience rather than a happy, joyous, victorious one? This book gives clear, detailed Scriptural help on all these subjects, and many more. *259 pages.*

The Christian Example

"The inspiring stories and articles are so encouraging and helpful in my daily life." California

"Thank you for your help through the *Christian Example* in leading a seeker to Christ." G.A., Pennsylvania.

"*TCE* is the purest periodical for youth that we know of." F.B., Kentucky

"I appreciate the high standards of the disciplined life of the Christian, stemming from the vital life and communion in Christ with practical obedience which is repeatedly set forth in *TCE*." J.M., Tennessee

The Christian Example is a 16-page biweekly publication, featuring factually based articles, poems, and stories that illustrate and develop Scriptural convictions in growing Christians.